INTO THE LIGHT

PREFACE

I can take no credit for these words. There are times when the words come rushing into my mind and I have to write them down. This sometimes happens at odd times, when I'm trying to sleep, trying to watch a movie or sometimes when I'm in the shower getting ready for work in the morning. Often the words are inspired by a sunrise, a beautiful sight, a word in a Sunday talk or a phrase from a hymn. It often surprises me when I go back and read these poems. I often think to myself, "where did that come from" or "did I really write that?" I can only thank my Father in Heaven for inspiring these words and making them known to me through the Holy Ghost. I hope that they bring you peace and happiness.

Some of these poems refer to light, some to the beauty of the earth and some are just random thoughts that have entered my strange mind at different times. They contain the heart of my testimony of Jesus Christ as our Savior and Redeemer. They contain my testimony of our Father's great Plan of Salvation. They contain my most heartfelt feelings about the world around me.

As always there is section entitled "Especially for Latter-day Saints. This section holds poems that speak of my testimony of the restored Gospel.

My only hope is that these words bring you peace. If I can turn one heart to the Savior, Jesus Christ then I have done some good in this life.

Doctrine and Covenants Section 4:4

For behold the field is white already to harvest; and lo, he that thrusteth in his sickle with his might, the same layeth up in store that he perisheth not, but bringeth salvation to his soul;

LIGHT OF THE WORLD

THIS SECTION OF POEMS ALL HAVE SOMETHING TO DO WITH LIGHT. I HOPE THEY BRING YOU PEACE AND POINT THE WAY TO THE LIGHT OF THE WORLD OUR SAVIOR, JESUS CHRIST.

INTO THE LIGHT

When I'm feeling like the darkness
Fills up my heart and mind
And it seems that sadness
Is all there is to find
Where can I look for something
To lift me from that gloom
To bring me joy and happiness
To brighten up the room
It seems the darkness deepens
As the shadows in the night
Nowhere can I even see
A simple ray of light
When the night is deepest
And I feel I've reached the end
A still, small voice whispers softly
You always have a friend
Someone who will listen
To every doubt and fear
Someone who will hold you close
Someone who's always near
You only need to ask Him
As you kneel in humble prayer
Our Savior knows your every doubt

Always He'll be there
To drive away the darkness
And guide you to the light
Waiting there with open arms
And smile shining bright.

PATHWAY TO THE LIGHT

In my early days at school
I shed many bitter tears
Wondering if it was worth it
Facing my childhood fears
How I longed for a friendly face
A kind smile to make my day
As I trod those shadowed halls
In despair I made my way

There were those who bullied
And filled my nights with fearful dreams
Who left me feeling empty
And alone or so it seems
I went through each and every day
Wondering when it all would end
Feeling that I was worthless
That I'd never find a friend

Then one day a kindly smile
Would light the way before
Some kind soul would show they care
And open up another door

Then the day was brighter
And the sun seemed yet to shine
I would have a bright new hope
Feeling the future was all mine

But those days were very few
And seemed so far between
Then I would once again descend
Into that world unseen
Wondering if it was worth it
Struggling through another day
Where would I find the courage
To go on along my way

Now looking back with wider eyes
I see the past was not so bad
I had family and loved ones
I feel blessed with what I had
Now I see those darkened days
Were a pathway to the light
Looking back in hindsight
My life was good and bright.

ANOTHER YEAR

Another year has passed me by
Yet the future looks so bright
Another year of my life
A step closer to the light
Though I know not what life will bring
But my happiness is complete
As I look into the future
I know I've lived a life so sweet

OUR CONSTANT SOURCE OF LIGHT

When the night seems dark and long
When it's hard to see the light
When we look for day to come
But only see the night
When we seek hope for a brighter day
But the clouds dim our view
When the dawn seems far away
When we wonder what to do
When it seems our hearts are breaking
When bad news doth abound
It's time to change our viewpoint
It's time that we turn around
We must always look to the source
Of all that's good and bright
Our Savior even Jesus Christ
Is the constant source of light
By His light and influence
Through the dark we will be led
For He is always there for us
As He has always said
I am the truth, the way the light

These words ring in our heart
Turn your face to the light
And let the healing start.

DARKEST NIGHT

The trials that we face in life
Oft weigh upon our heart
But we know we'll overcome
If we will do our part
Have faith in our Savior
For He descended below them all
He will always bear us up
He will not let us fall
And when the night seems darkest
Through the gloom we see a light
A glimpse of our heavenly home
Shining oh so bright
Then lift your head up, hold it high
For this life is short and fleet
Then in our Father's kingdom
Our life will be complete

THAT FAR AND DISTANT SHORE

I feel my play's come to an end
And my life's stage is growing dark
I feel that there's a journey
Upon which I must soon embark

For I see a light shining glowingly
On some far and distant shore
I feel a yearning to follow the light
Toward that far off door

For I hear a voice that is calling me
From a place I once called home
It's telling me my time is near
When no more on earth I'll roam

But this selfsame voice bespeaks
Of the joy that is yet to be found
It speaks of a long and happy life
With love and beauty all around

I know that shore is beckoning me
Waiting for my return
And when the lights finally go dark
It is for that place I'll yearn

For now I'll seek out happiness
With my loved ones all around
Upon this beautiful terrestrial sphere
Where all I need is found.

Not sure why my mind has been filled with thoughts of adversity and strife lately. Things are actually going fairly well for us at the moment. Oh we always have our little trials each and every day just as everyone does but nothing big has darkened our path for a while. I hope that these thoughts don't mean something is coming that we can't see yet. Whatever comes I know that with the help of my Savior I will find the strength to make it through.

THE SOURCE OF LIGHT

When faced with trials in mortality
Do we hang our head and cry
Or do we move on with certainty
And hold our head up high
For how we face adversity
Is the key to eternal life
We must not let it weigh us down
This moment of toil and strife
For we know our Savior, Jesus Christ
Bore all our grief and pain
That He would have compassion
That we might live with Him again
So when life seems dark and dreary
Look to the source of the worlds light
When you see Him standing there
The night will then be bright.

HISTORY AND PATRIOTISM

THIS SECTION CONTAINS POEMS OF WORLD HISTORY OR PATRIOTISM TO OUR GREAT COUNTRY. I LOVE THIS COUNTRY AND CAN'T IMAGINE LIVING ANYWHERE ELSE IN THE WORLD. I PRAY FOR OUR COUNTRY CONSTANTLY THAT IT MIGHT BE PRESERVED AND PROTECTED.

I have never been a real political person. I'm not a big believer in right-wing or left-wing ideology. As I see what is happening in our country I wonder if there is a political solution. I see so many politicians who seem corrupt or just don't care about this country; so many who are only trying to further their own personal interests. I see billions of dollars being spent because of the hatred of one man who from what I saw did so much good for our economy and our country. I think the day will come when our Father in Heaven will have to step in and end this evil. I truly believe that the solution lies there, not through any politician or political party. We must return to worshiping Jesus Christ and our Father. This is what we need in our country. If you disagree feel free to unfriend me, that's your choice.

WHEN WILL THE EVIL END

I fear to watch the news each day
See our country falling apart
When I see the rampant corruption
It gives me an ache clear through my heart
Our once great country is being torn down
From within its very halls
We're being slowly divided
By high, unscalable walls
Neighbor against neighbor
Brother against friend
How long can our world last
When will the evil end
Then I kneel in humble prayer
To my Father up above
Asking Him to wrap us safe
In His eternal love
Then the Spirit whispers quietly
In His arms peace we'll find
Then I know who's in control
He speaks softly to my mind.

Every year on January 27th we commemorate one of the most horrendous injustices that happened in history. On that day the concentration camp at Auschwitz was liberated. It is a great day in history but came too late for many of the Jews who were murdered by the Hitler regime. Those who survived this great atrocity live as a testimony to the terrible events of those years known as the Holocaust.

REMEMBRANCE

Some say it did not happen
The murder of the Jews
But thousands faced a broken heart
When they heard the news
That their precious loved ones
In the night were gone away
And in the concentration camps
How many would die today
The tattooed numbers on their arm
Are the survivors legacy
Proof of this injustice
That anyone can see
For the millions of innocent lives
Lost so long ago
This is a day of remembrance
So hang your head so low
And remember those who lost their lives
And those who lived in fear
May we never, ever forget
And for them shed a tear.

THE BEST OF THE BEST

This is for the veteran's
Heroes one and all
Where would our country be today
If they did not stand tall

To protect our freedom
And fight for those oppressed
These brave men and women
The best of the best

So today we honor you
The brave and the strong
Who in far and distant lands
Have fought for so long.

This election year has been a strange one. I don't know who is right and who is wrong or if there is a right and wrong. I only see the country that I love torn apart. I don't know who to believe or who to trust. I can only pray that whoever is elected president of this great land will have the people's best interests at heart. I can only place my trust in my Heavenly Father knowing that He is in control.

KNOWING HE IS THERE

As our great land is ripped apart
By forces beyond our ken
We ask why these times have come
Will they stop and when

These times have been predicted
By prophets long foretold
For many years we have been warned
For decades we've been told

The time is not far distant
When our Savior will soon reign
Then the earth will be reborn
We will see peace again

Until that time we live in faith
And kneel in humble prayer
To our Father up above
Knowing He is there.

CAN DEMOCRACY SURVIVE?

Last night I dreamed a marvelous dream
I saw those who've come before
Who left their life and homeland
For that far and distant shore
Where they would start a great new life
In the land of liberty
Free from dark oppression
Brought on by tyranny
Free to make their way in life
Where hard work would pave the way
Where through their own ingenuity
They could see a brighter day
In the land of promise
Far across the sea
They came to find a better life
In the land of the free

Some left their home and families
To seek the way of light
In those alabaster cities
In the distance shining bright
They went with little on their backs

With hope their only friend
With the strength to never break
But in the wind to bend
They settled in the cities
In the east and in the west
They came to build a better place
They came to join the best
Here they found the freedom
For which some would give their life
So that we who came abaft
Might live free from strife

Now I see our wonderful country
Torn and cut asunder
I wonder can we yet survive
Or is democracy going under
I wonder what the good brave souls
Who helped to build this nation
Think of what is happening
To their marvelous creation
Are they looking down from heaven
As down their cheek falls a tear
When they look upon the evil
That is spreading hate and fear
Is there something we can do

To stop the evil that we see

For I can assure you

It comes for you and me

MUSIC

MUSIC HAS ALWAYS PLAYED A BIG PART IN MY LIFE. I FOUND VERY EARLY IN LIFE THAT I LOVE TO SING. DURING THE YEARS WHEN I DIDN'T ATTEND CHURCH MUCH EACH SUNDAY I WOULD GO WITH MY AUNT, UNCLE AND GRANDMOTHER ON A SUNDAY DRIVE. WE WOULD SING THE HYMNS OF THE GOSPEL AND MANY OTHER SONGS. WHEN I GOT TO JUNIOR HIGH SCHOOL I HOPED TO JOIN THE CHOIR BUT WAS DISAPOINTED BY A TEACHER WHO FOR SOME REASON JUST DID NOT LIKE ME. IT WASN'T UNTIL MY SENIOR YEAR OF HIGH SCHOOL THAT ANOTHER TEACHER WHO TOOK A CHANCE ON A SHY, UNPOPULAR BOY AND ASKED HIM IF HE WOULD LIKE TO BE IN CONCERT CHOIR. THAT MADE MY SENIOR YEAR OF HIGH SCHOOL VERY SPECIAL AS I FINALLY FELT THAT I WAS A PART OF SOMETHING.

I would like to preface this next poem with a story that happened to us years ago. My mother-in-law passed away in 1991 after a along battle with cancer. They lived in Idaho at the time and Linda and I went up to Idaho and stayed at their home to help her dad prepare for the funeral. The day after we arrived Linda woke up with a song in her mind. She could hear it as plain as plain but couldn't remember the name of the song. She found a hymn book and after searching she found the song. That song was "Because I Have Been Given Much". This became a favorite song of ours. In December of 1994 we were touring the Bountiful temple prior to it's dedication in January. As we toured the beautiful temple we could hear the organ in the chapel playing. As befitting the Christmas season the songs we could hear were songs of Christmas. Then just as we got to the door of the chapel one song ended and the organist began a new song. That song was "Because I Have Been Given Much". We felt that Linda's mother was there in the temple that day and perhaps even inspired the organist to switch from her current repertoire of Christmas music to play that hymn just for us. It was a wonderful and spiritual experience.

MUSIC BEARS GREAT TESTIMONY

The hymns we sing each Sabbath day

Speak volumes to our heart

The music touches deep in our soul

It can help the healing start

They can bear strong testimony

Of our Savior dear

They invite the Holy Ghost

His whisperings we might hear

So sing the hymns of the gospel

Let the music fill your soul

The testimony that they bear

Will make your heart feel whole

MUSIC OF THE GOSPEL

The music of the gospel

Brings a spirit oh so sweet

It gives us comfort in our heart

It makes our life complete

When we sing of Jesus Christ

Of His never ending love

Our voices are in harmony

With our Father up above

Showing Him our gratitude

Through music's humble prayer

That whispers to our very soul

And assures us He is there.

1I love the old cowboy songs. I know that may seem strange to those who have been raised on rock and roll, hip-hop and rap music. I love Marty Robbins, Roy Rogers, Dale Evans, Gene Autry and many others. I love to watch old westerns. I have a classic country station on Pandora that I listen to almost exclusively in my truck. These songs never grow old for me.

I LOVE TO HEAR A BALLAD

I love to hear a ballad

Of the wild, wild west

Of a brave Texas ranger

Who wore a star upon his vest

Who faced down the outlaw

The one with the lightning hand

Bringing law to the lawless

In a dry and desperate land

I love to hear a ballad

About cowboys, real men

Driving cattle along the trail

Fighting wind and rain back then

Spending the day in the saddle

And nights 'neath the stars above

Dreaming of going home again

To the one they truly love

I love to hear a ballad
For it is a story told
Tales pulled from yesteryear
That never seem to grow old
I sometimes sit and wonder
Of those simpler times gone by
And dream of living the rugged life
Then heave a heavy sigh

Was I born in the wrong time
Would I have been happy then
But alas we can't turn back the clock
And live our lives again
We must be thankful for what we have
What blessings have come our way
We know we're where we're meant to be
With the life we live each day.

ETERNITY

THIS GROUP OF POEMS ALL SPEAK OF ETERNITY. FOR WE KNOW OUR TIME UPON THIS EARTH IS LIMITED YET WE KNOW WE WILL LIVE AGAIN. FOR OUR ETERNAL SOUL, OUR SPIRIT, IF YOU WILL IS ETERNAL AND DOES NOT DIE.

TOGETHER EVERMORE

There is a sorrow that we feel
When a loved one's gone away
That fills our heart with sadness
Each and every day
Yet this long sleep that men call death
Is but for a little while
Through our Heavenly Father's plan
We can make it through this trial
For we know we'll be reunited
On that far and distant shore
Never again to be apart
Together evermore.

ETERNAL FRIENDSHIPS

There are those we meet in life

And just know 'twas meant to be

Though it may be a fleeting moment

It creates a lasting memory

Maybe just a casual glance

Or the flash of a friendly smile

We think of them fondly

Even after a long while

I believe they are those we met

Before we came to earth

In that former life we lived

Where we all showed our worth

When we see their face again

It is a long lost memory

I believe there are friendships

That last for eternity.

UNTIL WE MEET AGAIN

There are many that cross our path in life

They touch a place deep in our heart

They are always in our minds

Even when we are apart

Some we've known for many years

Some for just a day

Yet we feel their absence

When they are away

We feel an emptiness inside

Until we meet again

Then such happiness fills our life

What joy we'll feel then.

NO GREATER GIFT

I know that I'm not perfect
Nor will I ever be
But through Christ's great atonement
A brighter future I can see
For despite my imperfection
I know my effort will suffice
Thanks to our Father's wondrous love
And our Savior's sacrifice
I know that I can live again
For He died that we might live
And be wrapped in His loving arms
No greater gift could He give.

MISSING YOU

When the still small voice whispers
Speaking quietly to your soul
It can bring you peace of mind
When your heart's an empty hole
When you miss someone completely
Who has quietly flown away
The still small voice can whisper
Hope for a brighter day
When we are reunited
With those loved ones gone before
Somewhere beyond the sunset
We'll be happy evermore.

I get a little melancholy around the holidays as I guess a lot of people do. There are a lot of theories about why this happens such as the lack of daylight, the colder days and the depression that comes because you can't provide the holidays for your family that you wish you could. But for me there is another reason. On November 27, 1968, which that year was the day before Thanksgiving, my father passed away. I was twelve years old and never really got to know him very well. I know that he was one of the kindest men. He would often stop to help people on the side of the road or sometimes to pick up hitchhikers, especially if they were servicemen. I know he was always good to me. There was only one time that I remember him being really angry with me and I deserved it that night. I don't think he really understood me since he and I were quite different. I loved learning and reading and he never had those desires. His reading ability was limited but his heart held unlimited love for his family. I felt that even at the young age that I was. So I hope one day to sit and talk with him. I would like to know what he thinks of me. Did I make him proud or have I been a big disappointment? But most of all I just want to tell him I love him.

SECOND CHANCE

If you were given a second chance
To speak to one who's gone before
What would you say to that dear soul
Who's passed beyond that door

Would you tell them how you loved them
And missed them tenderly
Would you hold them close to your heart
And kiss them lovingly

Would you tell them how you missed them
And wished that they were here
Would you hold them in your arms
And maybe shed a tear

Would you speak of past regrets
Of dreams thrown by the way
Would you speak of times gone by
Of some far and distant day

Would ask them how they feel for you
Did you fail or are they proud
Do they never speak of you
Or do they shout your praises loud

I hope someday to have that chance
With those who've passed beyond that door
To ask them what their lives were like
When they lived before

And maybe learn at their feet
What life was all about
What joy will fill my aching heart
I know that without a doubt

GREENER PASTURES

They say the grass is always greener
And I suppose it does seem so
For when you're young and foolish
You just can't wait to grow
Another year older you will be
Then you can drive a car
When you turn sixteen years old
You know then you will go far
They say you are too young to wed
But you know she is the one
You hurry down that flowered aisle
In a moment it is done
Nine long months we have to wait
To see this tiny child
Kicking around in his mother's womb
So beautiful and mild
Then you see that tiny face
Peering at you from your arms
Not the son you were hoping for
But a daughter with all her charms
You turn your back for just a moment
And when you turn back around
You no longer see that tiny babe

But a young woman you have found
Then before you know it
Your hair is turning gray
Your joints begin to hurt and ache
Then there comes a day
When you know it's time to go
To greener fields beyond
You wish you were sixteen again
Then time breaks that mortal bond
Then you know t'was meant to be
For you have lived your life
Passing on to greener pastures
Where there is no toil and strife

GOD, OUR FATHER
HIS SON JESUS CHRIST
THE HOLY GHOST

OUR FATHER'S TENDER MERCIES

Our Father's tender mercies

Are all around to see

From the complexity of a snow flake

To the leaves upon a tree

From the sunlight in the sky

That sheds its warm bright glow

To the moon and stars that shine

Upon the glistening snow

The sun upon the water

The storm clouds gathering in the sky

The flash of an eagle's wing

As it soars so high

We only need to look around

At all that's touched by His great hand

From the mountains rugged sides

To the waves upon the sand

And know that He created

Through His never ending love

This earth that shows such beauty

And the heavens up above.

WHO CAN CONCEIVE THE MIND OF GOD

Who can conceive the mind of God

Who created this wonderful earth

That blossoms forth with beauty

And treasures of great worth

Vermilion cliffs stretch to the sky

Sprinkled with a blanket of white

Tiny diamonds blazing radiantly

All across a field of white

Who can conceive the mind of God

As they watch an eagle fly

From its perch high in a tree

As it soars in a bright blue sky

The sunlight shining off a wing

Or a feather dropped from above

Stirs within one such emotion

Reminds one of His great, great love

Who can conceive the mind of God
When we go forth to see
The creatures created by His hand
In all their variety
The earth's great beauty passing by
All creatures great and small
Who would dare to not believe in
A loving God who made them all.

THE HOLY GHOST IS OUR GUIDE

To gain a steady testimony
One must first believe
Then from the Holy Ghost
A witness you'll receive
You will feel a burning in your heart
A witness oh so sweet
Then deep down within your soul
A testimony complete
For the Holy Ghost is our guide
He will teach us truth and light
Then lead us to a future
In the distance shining bright.

WE WILL ALWAYS HAVE A FRIEND

When the storm clouds gather in the east
And there is darkness all around
When ne'er a ray of sunshine
Can anywhere be found
When the night is darkest
And there's hours 'till the dawn
You wonder if you'll find the strength
To ever carry on
Lift up your head to heaven
Pour out your soul in prayer
For our Father's watching
Know that he is always there
Even on our darkest days
We will always have a friend
To guide us through the darkness
Even to our journey's end.

FOR GOD SO LOVED THE WORLD.

JOHN 3:16,17

For God so loved the world

He sent His only Begotten Son

Even Jesus Christ

The great atoning One

For He came not to condemn

But to save the world from sin

To lead us back to heaven

And bid us enter in

For He brought us Father's love

To all who live on earth

That all mankind might recognize

The glory of His birth

That we might learn to follow Him

Learn and feast upon His word

For this babe who was born this day

Is Jesus Christ our Lord.

REACH OUT TO THE SAVIOR

As we reach out to our Savior
He stretches out his sacred hand
To give to us the strength we need
Against the storms of life to stand
As we reach out with our heart
To our Savior up above
He will always bless us
With His never ending love
So when we feel we're not enough
And our failings bring us grief
Reach out to our Savior
He will send comfort and relief

HOW DO WE SHOW OUR GRATITUDE

How do we show our gratitude
To our Father up above
For the many blessings given
For His eternal love

For He sent His first born Son
To live with men on earth
To live and suffer every ill
That all might know His worth

When in that sacred garden
The olive press, Gethsemane
He paid the price for all our sin
Then died to set us free

Upon that cruel, cruel cross He bled
Gave up His life and died
Father please forgive them
Were the words He cried

So show your great gratitude
Each and every day
That our Father's spirit
Might always show the way.

LOVE ONE ANOTHER

As our Savior, Jesus Christ
Prepared to leave His little band
He gave them a new commandment
As He stood upon the sand

"Love one another
As I have loved you"
This commandment stands today
It is what we should do

We should have love for everyone
All the children of our God
And make their pathways brighter
As they walk on mortal sod

That when we leave this world behind
And stand before the Lord
We will know we've done our best
To follow His sweet word.

THE MASTER HEALER

Our country is divided
Near to the point of war
We watch the news and wonder
How can we withstand much more

Both sides say that they are right
What voices should we follow
When the voices that we hear
All seem dead and hollow

Then a still small whisper
Comes stealing in the night
Listen to your faithful heart
And always choose the right

For if we follow our Savior
Even Jesus Christ our Lord
May we ever follow Him
And listen to His word

For He is the Master Healer
Who can heal every ill
He can bring us peace and love
If we but do His will

THE GOOD SHEPHERD

The dark clouds gather on the mountain top
Touched red by the rising sun
With gladness we face the morning
As a new day has begun

Though the clouds are dark and drear
They cannot block out the dawn
For we know the sun will shine
And our mortal life goes on

For the source of truth and light
Goes before us every day
If we will but follow Him
The Good Shepherd will lead the way

WHERE TRUE HAPPINESS IS FOUND

We must look to the future
With hope for a brighter day
Pray our Heavenly Father
Will help us along the way

Through the bad and the good
With faith and charity
We must go ever onward
Toward eternity

For we cannot turn back the clock
To a day that's gone before
We can only look to the future
And know there's something more

Beyond this fragile, mortal sphere
The future looks so bright
When we follow in His footsteps
The source of truth and light

Father will not let us fail

If our faith in Him abound

It is in His royal courts above

Where true happiness is found

LET GOD PREVAIL

When we we turn our hearts to God
And say let God prevail
Then our lives are improved
The devil cannot assail
For our Father will protect us
With His spirit our hearts are filled
Upon this simple precept
A mighty fortress can we build
For when we say let God prevail
And give ourselves up to His will
Then the Spirit of the Lord
Will cause our hearts to thrill
We know that each and every day
Is a blessing sent from God
To ease our path along the way
While upon this earthly sod.

WE ALL FALL SHORT

As I wake up in the morning
With the rising of the sun
I thank my Heavenly Father
For a bright, new day begun
For the chance to try again
To live and learn and love
To take another step toward
My heavenly home above
And even when I fail
When my chance is looking grim
I know that through my Savior
I can return to Him
For we all fall short of glory
Alone we cannot stand
But through Christ's great atonement
We can find that promised land
Where we will live for all eternity
Surrounded by God's love
In those eternal halls of glory
In His mansion up above

Many times in my life I have felt "The Touch of the Masters Hand". I often feel it in my writing. I often feel it deep in my heart when I'm especially sad and sometimes even in my happiest moments. I promise you that if you seek out his touch, you can feel His hand in your life.

MASTER'S HAND

There is nothing that can heal
Like the touch of the Master's hand
For there is no greater help
Found throughout the land
For His touch can heal
Even the darkest night
His touch can soothe and comfort
Can make each day seem right
For the touch of the Master's hand
Can soothe all our care
For when we feel His healing touch
We rest assured that He is there

RETURN TO HIM

We lived before we came to earth
With our Father up above
Basking in the sacred light
Of His eternal love
Then we left those hallowed halls
A body we must gain
And learn of mortality
With all its joy and pain
That we might be found worthy
To return to Him someday
After we have lived our life
And followed along our way
Seeking out our Savior
Throughout mortality
That we might return and live with Him
Throughout all eternity.

WHISPERS

The Holy Spirit whispers quietly

That which helps us grow

Deep within our heart it speaks

That all truth we know

The Spirit testifies of Jesus Christ

That the enemy not deceive

Tells us we should show our thanks

For all that we receive

The Spirit whispers quietly

And if we heed with care

We can hear that whispered word

And know that God is there

Know of His Only Begotten Son who came

A dying world to save

It will whisper softly

"For you His life He gave"

He paid the price for all our sin

In the Garden Gethsemane

Then freely gave His life for us

And died upon that tree

So listen very carefully

To that voice so still and small

For the Holy Ghost will never lead astray

He whispers truth to us all

GIFTS

Our Father has given us unique gifts
Each of His children has their own
Look deep inside yourself
Your gift will become known
For some the gift of knowledge
While on this earthly sod
To some to know that Jesus Christ
Is the Son of God
Whatever gift you've been given
Is to help others along their way
So use those gifts to brighten
Some brother's darkest day
For if we help each other
Throughout mortality
We can make a heaven on earth
Seek out your gifts, you'll see

Saw a FaceBook post today about this scripture and then these words were leaping from my mind and onto the page.

Psalm 5:3

My voice shalt thou hear in the morning, O Lord; in the morning will I direct my prayer unto thee, and will look up.

AS I RISE TO GREET THE DAY

As I rise to greet the day
My mind turns to prayer
Again I speak with my Lord
Knowing that He is there
For I feel his presence
Deep within my heart
What a very lovely way
For the day to start
I know that He can hear me
And my request He will heed
For my Lord will never neglect
When I sincerely plead
Then throughout the day I go
With a prayer deep in my heart
That I might not stumble and fall
To the adversary's fiery dart
Then ere I lay me down to sleep
I seek the Lord again
To ask for His protection
'Til the morn should come and then
Once more I will seek my Lord
With the rising of the sun

As I kneel in humble prayer
And the new day has begun.

There is something that I have tried hard to learn throughout my life. When I was young I worried about what others thought of me. I was bullied and made to feel like my life didn't matter. I suffered through bouts of depression throughout most of my life. But now I know it doesn't matter anymore what others think. It only matters what I think of myself and what my Savior and my Father in Heaven thinks of me. Their opinion is the only one that matters. If there are those in your life who make you feel less than you are; if there are those who try to bring you down, don't listen to them. Only listen to that still small voice that will never tell you're not good enough.

WHEN OTHERS BRING US DOWN

It is sad that some you meet in life
Only want to bring you down
When your heart wants to smile
They do their best to make you frown
Their only real goal it seems
Is to bring you to your knees
When your heart wants to fly
There's only darkness that it sees
But we have a faithful friend
Who will never bring us low
For our Savior Jesus Christ
Will always love us so
He cares not whether rich or poor
Nor the countenance we bare
He only asks that we follow Him
Know that He is always there
Put our Savior first in life
Don't let others bring you down
Then in your heart will always be
A smile not a frown.

OPEN THE PATHWAYS OF HEAVEN

Our Savior taught this wonderful truth
For our enemies we should pray
That we might find forgiveness
Each and every day
For prayer opens up the door
That Father's blessings freely flow
To help us travel down the path
As through each day we go
To keep the windows of heaven open
That we are blessed by His great love
As we open up the pathways
To His Royal courts above

BOUNTEOUS BLESSINGS

When I sit and ponder

MY great blessings through the years

The gratitude I feel

Often brings my eyes to tears

For my Father in Heaven

Has blessed me bounteously

With the gospel in my home

With joy and family

With a knowledge of my Savior

And of His eternal love

That rains down marvelous blessings

From His Royal courts above

Material wealth means nothing

I have sufficient for my needs

I know that my fervent prayer

My Father always heeds

When my mortal life is over

And my final race is run

I know the blessings that He gives

Will have only just begun.

OUR FAITHFUL FRIEND

As we travel through this life
Down that ever changing path
There are times when tears will fill our eyes
There are times when we will laugh
But through it all we have a friend
We'll not walk the path alone
There is one who's by our side
For our sins He did atone
He makes the good days sweeter
The bad days fade away
As with our Savior we walk the path
Each and every day
He lifts us up when we are down
And soothes our troubled heart
He eases the most troubled soul
And lets the healing start
He is the source of light and truth
The resurrection and the life
He can bring us sunshine
As we walk through toil and strife
For He is the man of sorrows
Who upon the cross did die
Yet rose again on the third day

The grave He did defy
This man's name is Jesus Christ
He is our faithful friend
He will walk close by our side
Even to the bitter end

WHEN IN TIMES OF TROUBLE

When in times of trouble
When you are feeling down and low
Know that there is someone
Who will always love you so
When you feel discouraged
And your life seems out of place
Know that there is someone
Who saved the human race
He came to save the world from sin
His life He freely gave
That mankind might not be subject
To the finality of the grave
Because he had power over death
We know we will rise again
To live for all eternity
What joy we will know then
When in our Father's kingdom
In His royal courts above
Living in the shadow
Of His everlasting love

I have been pondering a lot lately about the relationship between myself and my children. I often wish it were a closer relationship but it seems life always gets in the way. It may seem strange to anyone who reads my poems but I have a hard time expressing my feelings out loud. I hold too much inside. I just hope that my children and my grandchildren know the tears I have secretly cried and still cry for them. Sometimes in the dark of night, sometimes in the light of day I hope they know they are never far from my thoughts as we are never far from Father's.

INFINITESIMAL LOVE

There is a special relationship
Between a father and a child
Hands that are rough from work
Become so gentle and mild
When a father holds his baby
It touches deep within his heart
You feel that special bonding
That lets love truly start
Then as the child grows tall and strong
The father swells with pride
Even though there are times
It becomes a bumpy ride
A father never turns his back
He feels no regrets
But only love and happiness
The older the child gets

So it is with Father in Heaven
He watches as we grow
He never will give up on us
As we wander to and fro
He only looks at us with pride

With an infinitesimal love
That rains down His blessings
From His royal courts above
His heart might ache as we go astray
Fills with joy when we repent
For our Father loves us all
We are His children heaven sent
Then when our mortal life is o'er
And our final race we've run
Then we can return to Him
When our journey here is done.

Many years ago my grandmother gave me a book written by Nephi Anderson. That book was called "The Castle Builder". The book follows Harald as he grows from boyhood to manhood in Norway. Harald is raised in the religion of the day until an uncle dies in a fishing accident. This uncle believed in the Bible and read it all the time. He disagrees with some of the things that the church taught so the local priest refuses to give him a "Christian burial". Harald begins to have his own doubts about some of the things that he has been taught. One night he has a dream where he is standing on a hill looking down into a valley. He sees endless lines of people entering this valley and realizes that they are his Viking ancestors. These men and women who were all strong and good never had the chance to hear about Jesus Christ. If what the church teaches is true all of these men and women would be condemned to hell just because they never heard of the Savior. This leads Harald to begin a journey which eventually leads him to a missionary of The Church of Jesus Christ of Latter-day Saints. After this missionary teaches him of the Plan of Salvation, Harald realizes it must be true otherwise God would be a very unjust God. He gives up nearly everything in his life to join the church. It is a wonderful book and has a love story in it as well. This wonderful plan provides a way for all of Father's children to be saved as we know those who did not have a chance to hear of the Gospel on earth will be taught in the life hereafter and given the chance to choose for themselves. This is why temple work and family history are so important.

ALL MUST MAKE THE CHOICE

Of the millions who've lived on earth

How many heard not the voice

Of our Savior, Jesus Christ

Had no chance to make a choice

How many never had the chance

To read His sacred word

How many would be condemned to hell

Simply because they never heard

Would a loving Heavenly Father

Not provide a simple plan

To save all of His children

Every woman and every man

For the Savior spoke of other sheep

That He said would hear His voice

Giving all the opportunity

To hear and make the choice

Whether they would follow Him

Or choose to turn away

This gives hope to many

And shows us all a brighter day

RANDOM THOUGHTS

THIS SECTION OF POEMS ARE JUST RANDOM THOUGHTS I HAVE HAD. SOME ARE RELATED TO THE GOSPEL SOME ARE NOT. I HOPE YOU ENJOY THEM.

HOW CAN WE TEACH OUR CHILDREN

How can we teach our children
In life there's no free ride
Only hard work and industry
Can ever turn the tide

How can we teach our children
To trust our Father up above
To put ourselves in His great care
And trust in His eternal love

How can we teach our children
Of Jesus Christ, our Savior dear
And of His eternal sacrifice
That made the way so clear

Only through example
And with love unfeigned
Can we show our children
How salvation is obtained

For our children are always watching
Everything we do and say
We must be a living example
Each and every day

THIS WONDROUS CREATION

Have you ever sat and pondered
Around a campfire late at night
Beneath a beautiful ebony sky
With a million stars shining bright

Have you ever watched the sunrise
Over purple mountains high
Or wondered at an eagle
As it soared across the sky

Have you ever seen a sky so blue
That your mind can't comprehend
Or looked upon a forest of trees
That you're sure will never end

Have you stood upon a lofty peak
Looked to the valley below
Or wondered at the beauty
Of the white and falling snow

For the wonders of this earth
Are beautiful to behold
Like a flowing tapestry
With colors bright and bold

This wondrous creation
Shaped by God's omnipotent hand
I'll never tire of the wonders
All across this stunning land.

I saw a quote today that said:
"Don't let the entire staircase overwhelm you. Just focus on that first step."
Of course there was a poem in there somewhere.

THE BOTTOM OF THE STAIRS

When standing at the bottom step

Of a staircase you must climb

Do not be discouraged

Just give yourself some time

For it may not be just what it seems

Each step will bring you near

To the end of your journey

So step upward without fear

Though the steps seem high and steep

At the bottom of the stair

They may grow much easier

Once you see what's really there

The first step is the hardest

Yet climb the stairs we must

With the final goal in mind

In our ability we should trust

And when we reach the final step

We'll know we paid the price

Then know that the journey's end

Was worth the sacrifice

THE NEW YEAR BEGINS

As the old year ends and the new begins
Let us look not to the past
Let us look forward to the future
To those things we know will last

For our families are forever
This truth we cannot deny
For our Father has told us so
And we know He does not lie

So keep your family close by your side
Let them feel your love
Show them that you know the truth
Of your heavenly home above

Help them to see the light
That shines bright everyday
And leads us to our Father's home
And will always show the way

This might seem a little different but there is something I am thankful for. For years I struggled with how to convey my thoughts and my testimony to others. Then one day words began to form in my mind. They came out in the form of a rhyme. From that day forward I have had words come to my mind that have helped to express my feelings for the gospel and to share my testimony. I thank my Heavenly for giving me this outlet, for it has come to mean so much to me. I am grateful for all the wonderful comments I have received from so many of you. I am grateful for this blessing that I know my Heavenly Father has given me.

FOCUS ON THE GOOD IN LIFE

Don't focus on the negative
But on the blessings in your life
Look for the tender mercies
Don't focus on the strife

Look for those great blessings
Sent from Father above
The flowers and the trees and birds
All are prove of His great love

So focus on the good in life
There is beauty all around
When we allow our eyes to focus
Happiness can be found.

MAY OUR HEARTS BE FILLED WITH GRATITUDE

May our hearts be filled with gratitude
For the promise of each day
May thank Him for the gospel
That shows to us the way

May we thank our Heavenly Father
For the blessings he will send
For He blesses us every day
'Til our mortal life with end

Then those blessing continue
Throughout all eternity
As we share eternal life
With friends and family

Showing our great gratitude
In all we do and say
For every tender mercy
He has sent along the way.

There have been many miracles in my life. I was a determined bachelor. Girls scared me and I couldn't talk to them. Then I met an amazing girl who brought me out of my shell and we fell in love and were married. We wanted children but it looked like it was not going to happen. It was nearly 5 years after we were married that our oldest son was born. I consider him a miracle as we were told by some doctors that my wife would never be able to conceive. Then a 2nd miracle came along 8 years later and we were blessed with twins. Now we have 3 granddaughters and 3 foster grandkids that I have come to care for and will miss them when they go back to their mother. I have seen so many miracles that I can't even name them all. Just look around and you will see that you too have seen miracles.

MIRACLES

Do you believe in miracles
In our modern day
They are happening all around us
Or so some people say

I believe in miracles
For I have seen them in my life
I have seen miracles happen
Even during times of strife

Don't stop believing in miracles
We all must do our part
To be a miracle in someone's life
And let the healing start

THANKFULNESS

In great thankfulness this day
I humbly bow my head
Give thanks to thee my Father
For my daily bread
For the beauty of this earth
Which everywhere abound
For the joy and happiness
That is shown all around
For the very air we breathe
For friends and family
For the knowledge that we have
Truths of eternity
My thanks to thee I freely give
Yet I know 'tis not enough
For again you bless me
When life seems so rough
And yet I feel thy loving arms
Around me every day
Taking me by my wayward hand
And showing me the way.

This past year I read Richard Paul Evans newest book called THE NOEL LETTERS. As one of the chapter headings he had put this quote.

"A BLANK PIECE OF PAPER IS GOD'S WAY OF TELLING US HOW HARD IT IS TO BE GOD."
  -   SYDNEY SHELDON

As I thought about this quote these words were tumbling down the hill of my consciousness and spilling out onto the page. No matter how hard it is, carry on each day. God will not leave your pages blank.

THE BOOK OF LIFE

We all start out an empty page
Our story filled in by life
As each day passes and we grow
The page is filled with joy and strife

For the author of our life
Is our Father up above
He fills up each and every leaf
With words of comfort and love

Then when the story's over
And at the end we've come
What a marvelous book we'll be
When our Father calls us home

ALONE AND AFRAID

There are those who are lonely
Even in a crowded place
They hold their head up proudly
With a smile upon their face

But deep inside their heart is breaking
They feel scared and alone
They feel the sadness deepen
And inside they hide a groan

For they walk in silent dread
Crying oceans of silent tears
They never feel they're good enough
They live only in their fears

So look around you every day
You know not who needs your aid
Just show a little kindness
For this you will be paid

Not with monetary value
But through kindness you may start
To open up a heavy door
And touch on someone's heart.

THAT I MAY BE FOUND WORTHY

Oh my Father I know what I am
A man often filled with sin
To many times I locked the door
And failed to let my Savior in

But I strife every day
To change within my heart
That I might be found worthy
That I have done my part

That one day soon I'll prove my worth
In every thought and deed
That I might then help my brother
Who I see in his need

With faith in my Savior
I will go forward every day
Knowing that He paid the price
That He came to show the way

Then maybe when my life is over
And my final race is won
That I might be found worthy
When my mortal life is done

A PRECIOUS THING

A testimony is a precious thing
We hold sacred in our heart
It will grow piece by piece
If we but do our part
Read our scriptures
Work and pray
Help our brother along the way
Do our best to follow Christ
Hold to the iron rod
Learn and live His word each day
While on this mortal sod
Then in our hearts our testimony
Will ever stronger grow
It will fill our heart and mind
Of this we surely know.

This one has a lot of special meaning for me for I seldom like what I see when I look in the mirror. I often have to tell myself that this reflection that I see is just that, a reflection of my outer self, nothing more. It does not show what is in my heart. I have to remind myself that I am a child of God, heir to His kingdom where, if I pass this mortal test, I will live with Him again as I did before I came to this mortal sphere. I hope all of you will look past the dark reflection you see in the mirror and look at the enlightened being deep within. That is who you truly are.

THE MIRROR

Sometimes we look into a mirror
We may not like what we see
But the eyes that we are using
May be the eyes of an enemy

Do not believe the lies it tells
This mirror hanging on the wall
But look deep within your heart
At the spirit standing tall

For what we see in the looking glass
Is what we see with mortal eyes
But our Father in Heaven knows
That we can win the prize

For He looks within the heart
And sees what lies within
Don't let the mirror convince you
That the battle you can't win

Look past that dark reflection
At the warrior deep inside
Then go forth with mighty courage
Knowing you can turn the tide.

IN NEED OF RESCUE

There are those in need of rescue
In the sphere in which we live
Take the time to reach out your hand
Take the time to give

When we reach out to help another
Then our testimony grows
We know not the one that we might help
Or what seeds we sow

For the ground of a person's heart
Changes with the years
It may be that the one you help
Is shedding silent tears

Look around you as you pass
Through each and every day
There are those in need of rescue
That you might show the way.

WHEN WE FACE OUR MOUNTAIN

When we face our mountain
Who will help us climb
When we struggle up that final hill
Who will take the time

Sometimes friends will lift you up
While others will pull you down
Some will make you smile wide
Others only make you frown

We all have our mountains
And it's uphill all the way
But when we reach that summit
We can see a brighter day

Don't heed those who add their woes
To the burden you must lift
But look to those who ease your load
They are such a special gift

So when the way ahead seems steep
And the trail seems much too long
Look for those who've gone before
Their faith can make you strong

When you at last reach that peak
Look back for those behind
There are always those who need your help
Keep them always in your mind

For you'll never know the one you help
Might be your truest friend
So help your brother along his path
'Til we all reach the final end.

We watched a movie on Disney+ called "CLOUDS". It's a good movie and very sad. As I watched it I suddenly felt the urge to write these words. No spoilers, you have to watch the movie yourself if you get the chance. Just make sure you have that box of Kleenex handy, you'll need it.

AROUND THE BEND

As we walk down mortality's path

We must live day by day

For tomorrow is not promised

Or at least that's what they say

But when we look into eternity

Our lives need never end

For when we leave our life behind us

When we pass around that bend

When our mortal life is over

Our spirit will live on

So I ask you not to shed a tear

If you wake and find me gone

Just know I've gone to pave the way

Down that path we all must trod

The path toward eternity

When we leave this mortal sod.

GOD'S ARTISTRY

The beauty of God's artistry

Is all around upon this earth

There is beauty in the flowers bloom

And in a baby's birth

For God's palette is unending

The colors bright and bold

Seeing the work of His mighty hand

Will never fade or grow old

The green of pines on the mountainside

The red rock spires below

The colors of the rising sun

The mountains touched with snow

All His works are beautiful

Just look and you will see

How the beauty of this bounteous earth

Shows His glorious artistry

In the last year we have had the opportunity to have three foster children living with us. It is a sad story that I can't really go into but they were homeless when they came to us. It has been a crazy year. There have been ups and downs. There have been times when I wanted to just hug them and tell them it will be alright and times when I would have liked to punish them. The greatest punishment you could give these three children was to take their phones away. They played games and watched videos constantly and if they didn't have their phone they didn't know what to do with themselves. Through it all they found a way into our hearts. They have now gone back to live with their mother again. I sit here and shed tears of joy for them and sadness for us because we will miss them. Their mom says we can have them come over for sleep overs on the weekends so there is that to look forward to Sebastian, Janna, Deklan we will miss you and we wish you the best.

CHILDREN

It seems that children have way
To steal away your heart
You try to keep your distance
You try to do your part
There are times when they annoy
And you wish they weren't so loud
Then there are other times
When they just make you proud
You try to help them through their problems
That they might learn to deal with life
For you know what's ahead
You have seen the toil and strife
But in the end the choice is theirs
They must find their own true way
All you can do is watch them grow
And always for them pray.

FAMILY TIES

There is nothing to compare
To the joy of family all around
For there, we can be ourselves
Let our love abound
There is no greater joy in life
Than the wonderful family ties
To see our posterity
Right before our very eyes
So when the storm clouds gather
And it seems you just might drown
When you feel that all is lost
Do not wear a frown
Turn to your family
In their arms, comfort find
For the love of a family
Brings you peace of mind
For a family's sacred love
Will last through eternity
This is love that will never end
This is a sacred certainty

Due to age, arthritis and the disappointment of not having anyone to hunt with I don't get out much anymore. But I miss it with all my heart. As the fall approaches I still plan in my mind where and when I would hunt. There is nothing to make the heart race like having a pheasant flush from right under your feet or a rabbit burst from cover when you least expect it. There is no other activity that makes you feel more alive than stalking a herd of elk and knowing that they are near and then hearing that bugle so close it stops you in your tracks. I can think of nothing more beautiful than the sunrise over the marsh with the sky filled with ducks and geese as you await the daylight to take that first shot. The thrill you feel as you sit and glass a distant hillside and then, seemingly from out of nowhere, a big buck appears. There are times the feelings overwhelm me and I shed a tear for those lost years that are now just a distant memory.

THE HEART OF A HUNTER

The majestic sound of a bugling elk
As he calls his harem home
The sunlight on a mule deer's tines
As through the sage it roams
The sudden explosion of beating wings
As a pheasant bursts from the ground
The cacophony of ducks and geese
In the marsh all around
The thrill of a rabbit as it bursts
From it's well concealed place
These are sights and wonderful sounds
That make the heart of a hunter race
The kill is anticlimactic
Of our skill we do not boast
For to be out in nature
Is what really matters most
I hope that when my life grows dim
And I know the end is near
I want the sound of bugling elk
To be the melody that I hear.

For the last two days there have been the most beautiful sunrises. I see them as I am driving to work in the morning and it's all I can do to keep my mind on my driving. The colors are indescribable. Red, orange and shades of gray and black; then the purple of the mountains in the foreground is a wonderful sight. If you haven't experienced it I would suggest you wake up early, put your daily cares aside and just watch the sunrise. It will make the rest of the day pale by comparison and make you thankful to be alive.

THE BEAUTY OF CREATION

When the beauty of a sunrise
Rivals anything you've seen
When you watch an eagle or a hawk
Sit on a branch and preen
When you see a mighty mountain elk
Steal silently through the trees
When you watch a mighty rain storm
Move across the dark, gray seas
When you know that all this beauty
Could not come along by chance
Then let your heart leap with joy
Let it sing and dance
For a hand that is mightier
Than the hand of man
Created the beauty of this earth
As only a loving Father can
He created all you see
The moon and stars above
He did this as a Father would
To prove His never ending love

So before you lay your head at night

Upon that pillow sweet

Give thanks to your Father

Who has made your life complete

He who created all

The beauty that you see

Who painted the bright sunrise

Also created you and me

He gave to us this beautiful place

To live out our mortal probation

That the beauty of the earth

Fills our hearts with great elation

Yet when our mortal life is over

When no more on earth we trod

We know a place of greater beauty

Elevated from this earthly sod

Where we will dwell with Father

And Jesus Christ our Lord

Basking in the brightness

Of His everlasting word

QUESTIONS

What do others see in you
When they look into your eyes
Do they see the Light of Christ
Shining bright as clear blue skies
Do they see His countenance
When they look into your face
Do they feel a little brighter
As they face the human race
When they pass you on the street
Do they put on a happy smile
Do you bring them gladness
If even for a little while
If you can honestly answer yes
To the questions posed above
Then you are on the narrow path
That leads to the Savior's love
When I ponder for myself
I still have a ways to go
I just keep trying everyday
To always make it so.

We have had a number of quail living in our neighborhood. There are about six or eight pair of male and female. I expect we will soon be seeing some little ones running around too. This morning as I walked out the door there was a big ole male bird sitting in our driveway. He let out his raucous call just as I walked out the door. I guess he was as startled as I was. He turned and ran for the cover of the trees and I just stood and wondered at the beauty all around me. These words came to my mind.

QUAIL'S CALL

I'm greeted by a quail's call
As I step out of my door
In the early morning light
Who could ask for more
The sun breaks o'er the mountains peak
It spreads its rays around
Putting the shadows on the run
As it chases them 'cross the ground
The morning air is brisk and cool
As it brushes 'cross my face
I look up to the mountains high
Thank God for this beautiful place
Here among the mountains tall
In this valley is my home
Here I'll live my mortal life
Never more to roam
And when my time on earth is through
All I ask my friend
Is that you lay my body down
When my path comes to it's end
Where the quail sings his song
And the sun spreads forth its light

Shining down upon me

With its rays so bright.

THE ROAD TO HAPPINESS

Ofttimes the road to happiness
Is a rough and rocky path
It sometimes seems we just can't win
We lose sight of what we hath
Yet if we follow the narrow way
That leads to eternity
Then whatever the road ahead
How happy we will be
For though the path that we might tread
Is filled with twists and turns
The road will seem much brighter
If for our heavenly home we yearn
So set your sights on the final goal
Seek heavenly help each day
For there are angels among us
To help us on our way

MYOPIC

We must not be myopic
In our view of eternity
For if we believe that mortal life
Is all that we can see
We limit the power of Father
To lead us through this mortal life
For we lose sight of eternity
Through the world's toil and strife
But if we allow our vision
See the path stretch out before
Ever onward to eternity
Through heavens open door
Then we will see the miracles
That our Father soon will send
For when our mortal life is over
'Tis the beginning not the end.

THE ROAD OF MORTALITY

I see before me a long, long road
That rolls out on and on
It is a road that I must walk
As each new day doth dawn

This road is paved with happiness
In places washed with tears
There are days I walk in sunshine
There are miles of my greatest fears

But at the end of this long, long road
I see the shining prize
It is at the end of the road
That I must turn my eyes

For there I see the Tree of Life
Shining brightly in the night
I long to partake of its wholesome fruit
As I strive to do what is right

We all must walk this long, long road
It is the road of mortality
Through our days of probation
We keep our eyes on eternity

With the iron rod of the gospel
To guide us through each day
We must hold fast with all our might
If we hope to find our way.

HELP OUR BROTHER

I believe we should help our brother
Who may have lost his way
We know not it might be us
On some far and future day
We may need a hand to lift us up
Someone to show they care
A friend to lend a helping hand
Their crust of bread to share
So as you travel down the path
Look around for those in need
For if you help another
You will gain a friend indeed

JUST BEYOND THAT DOOR

When I stand upon a pinnacle

And look at the sight below

My heart swells with gratitude

For it is then I truly know

Our Father in Heaven gave us this earth

With its beauty all around

We only need to look and see

The wonders that abound

The color of the bare rock walls

That fades into the trees of green

The blue of an autumn sky

No greater beauty have I seen

To spy an eagle flying

Higher than the eye can see

Knowing that he soars alone

With a yearning to be free

The sunlight upon the water

As it sparkles and it shines

To spy a deer or mighty elk

Strolling through the pines

This is what makes life worth living

In this terrestrial world below

For greater beauty awaits us
This in my heart I know
When we return to our heavenly home
To greet those who've gone before
Sights beyond imagination
Wait just beyond that door

This one is very personal. I debated whether to even post this but I felt some strange compulsion to do so. You see on Saturday, September 19, 2020 Linda and I will have been married for 45 years. It was a beautiful, sunny Saturday morning when we went to the Salt Lake Temple and were joined together for time and all eternity. I love her today as much as I did that Saturday morning 45 years ago.

I STILL RECALL THE DAY

I still recall the day we met
It seems like yesterday
You laughed at my silly joke
I felt I'd lost my way
The days and weeks and months passed by
We had good times and some bad
We sat and talked of a future
What crazy dreams we had
Then when I popped the question
I was sure my heart you'd hear
Beating loudly in chest
Feel me shivering with fear
Then I heard the answer
I had waited for so long
When you said that simple word
I knew I was not wrong

Then our life began anew
Promised for eternity
In God's holy temple
We became a family
But the children did not come

We cried out faithfully
Praying for a miracle
We waited patiently
Then came the day God heard our prayer
A son was sent from heaven
Our family was now perfect
A miracle we'd been given
Then later we were blessed with twins
Such joy filled our heart
An eternal family we'd become
We will never be apart

Forty-five years ago this month
We knelt across that altar
Though our bodies are growing old
Our love will never falter
For we renew that love each day
Through words and through deeds
We do our best to help each other
And see to the others needs
When one of us must pass that veil
Cross to the other side
We know we will be together again
For eternity we'll abide
There in our Father's kingdom

I feel this certainty
Our love will there continue
Throughout all eternity

BE A LIGHT

In a world filled with darkness
With not an end in sight
When you feel you can't go on
Turn around and be a light
Share of your abundance
Give to someone in need
Then the world is a brighter place
If this message you should heed
And when your life seems darkest
And you've tried with all your might
Then turn to the Savior
The source of truth and light
He will brighten any day
When your burden's hard to bear
He will lend a helping hand
Know that He is always there.

This morning driving to work I saw the most beautiful sunrise. It wasn't long before these words came to my mind.

'NEATH THE MOUNTAIN SHADOW LONG

Salmon pink clouds

Against a pale blue sky

Fringed by purple mountains

Reaching up to the sky

As slowly the round yellow sun

Shows its brilliant face

My heart swells with gratitude

To live in this beautiful place

Where the purple mountain peaks

Dusted with their blanket of white

Stand out against the star-studded sky

On a clear and beautiful night

Where the full alabaster moon

Shows its face so bright and clear

Reach out your hand and touch it

It seems it is so near

Here I will spend my days

'Neath the mountains shadow long

Where the quiet beauty

Is as restful as a song.

CHRISTMAS

THIS SECTION CONTAINS POEMS OF CHRISTMAS AS WELL AS SOME STORIES OF MEMORIES FROM CHRISTMASES PAST. THESE ARE VERY DEAR TO MY HEART AS CHRISTMAS IS ONE OF MY FAVORITE TIMES OF THE YEAR.

This next one is very personal to me and I wondered if I should share but here it is. As many of you know my father died as the result of an industrial accident the day before Thanksgiving in 1968. Christmas that year was somewhat subdued and was a terrible day for my mother who was missing my dad so much. With insurance money and the help of relatives my mom had gone all out that year to give my younger brother and I everything we had asked for. I was so excited to see all of the gifts I had asked for and more, that in my foolish, childish mind I spoke words that caused my mom to shed tears. I immediately regretted what I had said and wished I could recall those hurtful words. That was the day I realized just how much we had lost and especially what my mom had lost. I truly regret the words I said that day and hope my mom forgives me and realizes that I was still just a child and spoke as a child.

CHRISTMAS REGRETS

This time of year is sometimes hard
When my heart is filled with regret
That the ghost of Christmas past
Just won't let me forget

Like Christmas day in '68
My mother was so sad
I saw her tears fall from her eyes
For she missed my dad

Then in my child's tongue I spoke
And caused more tears to fall
Saying that this Christmas
Was the best Christmas of all

When I saw the terrible anguish
On my mother's face
I wished I could recall those words
And return them to their place

Now that I am older
I know what I had done
And I hope she has forgiven me
Her young and wayward son

For I looked only at the things
That I received that year
Not thinking of what she had really lost
I was the reason for her tears

THE LIGHTS OF CHRISTMAS

Christmas is a marvelous time
When the world is filled with light
All around us we can see
Colored lights shining bright
Upon our Christmas tree they shine
And on every city street
Houses lit with shining lights
Oh what a beautiful treat

Remember what these lights are for
The tiny child born this day
A light shining in the darkness
To show mankind the way
For He is the source of truth and light
This child of humble birth
The lights we see at Christmas
Testify of His worth

THE MUSIC OF CHRISTMAS

The beautiful music of Christmas
Songs that celebrate His birth
Those that tell of the bright, bright star
That shown to all the earth
Songs that fill our hearts with joy
Of a babe in a manger lay
Music that brings us happiness
As we celebrate that sacred day
Music that tells of Mary
His mother who gave Him birth
Of the angels that spoke to the shepherds
Who testified of his worth
Songs that fill us with God's love
That He sent to earth that night
He gave His son to all mankind
A light shining oh so bright

THE DAY IT ALL BEGAN

As we prepare to celebrate

The tiny child born that day

We see the babe in the manger

Lying quietly in the hay

But our thoughts must also turn

To the child as He grew

For He came to save the earth

He came to save me and you

For our Savior grew in stature

He went about doing good

He healed the blind and the lame

As he grew to full manhood

Then in the garden Gethsemane

He paid the price of sin

Then died upon that terrible cross

The victory He would win

So as the day approaches

When we celebrate His birth

Remember this was just the start

Of His mission here on earth

For He suffered and He died

To fulfill His Father's plan

For He was the promised Savior

The one and only sinless man.

This is another memory of Christmas from my childhood. My mother loved Christmas and always made it special for us. The living room of our home had one wall covered with decorated mirror tiles. My mom believed this made the room look larger and in a way it did. Each year we would go shopping for a Christmas tree. It was always a large, full bodied tree, mostly a fir of some type. Then my mom would pay the tree lot to have the tree flocked white. We shopped at several places across the Salt Lake valley but there were a few I remember better than others. For several years my mom purchased the tree at Aoki's tree lot. This at first was just a small tree lot on 7th east and then later moved to a large nursery area on 39th south and just above 13th east. I remember the small lot on 7th east because we would go there and they would have barrels where they burned wood and they served hot chocolate and hot cider. It was always just a great time to go shopping for a Christmas tree. After the tree was purchased and flocked the tree lot would then wrap it in plastic and whoever in the family had a truck would load it up and take it to our home. For many years that person was me and I'll never forget how carefully we had to load and unload that tree so the flock wouldn't fall off.

When we got to the house we would place the tree right in front of the wall in the living room that was covered with the mirrors. This wall was directly across from the large front window so the tree was visible from the street. We would let the tree stand overnight and then decorate it the next day. Once the tree was decorated it made quite a spectacle when viewed through the front window. With the mirrors behind it the tree looked even bigger than it was. My mom worked at ZCMI in the Tiffin Room for many years and they used to have the Festival of Trees inside ZCMI. She would walk through the trees and get ideas on how to decorate our tree. I remember that for several years we would take 3 round ornaments and put a wide piece of ribbon through the hangers. Then we would tie the three ornaments to branches on the tree with a big bow.

The tree was always beautiful no matter what we did to it. By the time Christmas came and then New Years and we took the tree down it would leave a huge mess. Mom always cussed the mess the tree made but it didn't matter, the next year we would do it all again. Love those memories.

THE CHRISTMAS TREE

See the tree all shimmering

With brightly colored light

And a star atop the tree

Such a beautiful sight

The presents that are carefully placed

All around the tree

Wrapped in lovely paper

Make a beautiful sight to see

May we look to that long ago star

That led to the child that lay

In a lowly manger

On that first Christmas day

Though this year has been like no other in my memory we still have cause to celebrate. With so many sick with this crazy virus it may not seem like Christmas but it is still the season. We have said goodbye to many loved ones during the year yet through our Savior's love we know there is still hope for a brighter future. If you are sick with COVID or you have lost loved ones to this dreaded virus that has plagued us throughout the year, open your hearts to the Savior. Allow His love to enter in and heal you. I promise if you do this you will still find cause to celebrate. May we always remember the reason for the season. It is not what we receive but what we give to others that is important. Let your light shine out to all the world. Spread His gospel wide. For through His love we will be healed.

HE OPENED THE DOORWAY TO HEAVEN

Though we may not feel like celebrating

It has been a crazy year

Lift up your heads and shout

Be ye of good cheer

For the Savior came to earth

Upon this sacred day

To save all the world from sin

To show to all the way

So do not be discouraged

Keep your loved ones near

Celebrate within your heart
With those you hold so dear
For it's not what we receive
Celebrate what we've been given
The greatest gift to all mankind
Opened the doorway to heaven

MY SHRINKING CHRISTMAS LIST

As the years go swiftly by
And we grow old and wise
It seems that our Christmas list
Shrinks mightily in size

We begin to truly see
That what we really need
Cannot be bought in any store
No sparkling bauble or bead

But the love of family
Shining brightly all around
Being with those loved ones
Hearing the joyous sound

Of children as they look with wonder
At the gifts they've been given
We suddenly learn and realize
We've been given a piece of heaven

And so our greatest gift we've found

That money cannot buy
We feel this love swell in our hearts
And heave a happy sigh

For we know that we've found happiness
A piece of heaven here on earth
As we celebrate our Savior
And the day of his birth

With our family all around
With wonder in our heart
No greater gift could e're be given
No greater love impart.

MARY AND THE SHEPHERDS

The shepherds spoke out boldly
Of the beautiful sight
Of the angels they had seen
Singing loudly in the night
But Mary kept all these things
Deep within her heart
For she had also seen an angel
Who told her of her part
To bring this child into the world
Who was God's only begotten Son
He was the Savior of mankind
The great atoning one

THE GREATEST GIFT

As you consider gifts to give

To loved ones near and dear

Consider also a special gift

For Him who took away our fear

For the only gift He asks

Is a humble and contrite heart

To follow in His footsteps

To always do our part

So when you see these lovely gifts

Underneath the tree so bright

Remember our Savior who came to earth

To lead us back into the light

Offer up this gift to Him

Kneel in humble prayer

For He is the greatest gift

And He is always there.

THE CHILD BORN THIS DAY

A new star shone in the ebony sky

For the Child born this day

The Messiah who was foretold

Had come to show the way

Shepherds watched their flocks by night

Seated upon the ground

When the heavens opened

And light shown all around

An angel of the Lord appeared

And said "ye need not fear"

For I bring glad tidings

For all mankind to hear

For into you a child is born

To save the world from sin

He opened up the narrow way

And bid us enter in.

HOLIDAY BLUES

This time of year is difficult
In so many ways
So many people struggle
To make it through the days
To try to fulfill wishes
Though their own never do come true
Fills their heart with sadness
And chills them through and through
So look around this time of year
Be kind to those you meet
For we all experience heartache
With its sadness so complete

ESPECIALLY FOR LATTER-DAY SAINTS

It has always been my desire to take a church history tour. To go and stand in that sacred grove where the Father and Son appeared to Joseph Smith so long ago. I doubt I will ever make it there now but I can use my imagination.

SACRED GROVE

Today I stood on sacred ground

Where the Father and Son once trod

Where a confused and faithful boy

Once went to pray to God

For He knew that he lacked wisdom

And came to ask His Father above

Sure he would receive an answer

Trusting in his Father's love

For a marvelous work would soon come forth

Among the children of men

For the true gospel of Jesus Christ

Would be restored again.

FROM CUMORAH'S HILL

It was not a mighty mountain
Yet it brought forth such a thrill
When the plates were revealed
Upon Cumorah's hill

For God had chosen this humble mount
To show to men His will
When the Book of Mormon
Came forth from Cumorah's hill

Translated by the gift of God
That His spirit our hearts might fill
With the fullness of the gospel
That came forth from Cumorah's hill

IN A SACRED GROVE OF TREES

In a sacred grove of trees
A young man knelt in prayer
For He did not have a doubt
That His God was there
For the boy lacked wisdom
For which he'd come to find
Asking of his Father
Who he knew would be so kind
The forces of evil assailed him
There was darkness all around
The young man felt overwhelmed
And fell upon the ground
Then a light appeared to him
Sent the darkness fleeing away
There appeared two heavenly beings
To Joseph Smith that day
And so began the restoration
Of our Saviors church on earth
That all of Father's children
Might one day know his worth.

I woke up this morning with the image of bloody footprints in the snow and I wondered why that image came to mind. Then I remembered the story of the early Saints as they were forced from their homes in Missouri. It was the dead of winter and the mobs forced them out into the cold. Many left with little to protect them from the terrible cold. Many did not even have shoes. As they walked through the frozen snow it cut their feet and they left behind bloody footprints. In our warm and cozy world that we live in, even with the virus we are dealing with, I can't imagine what those early Saints went through.

BLOODY FOOTPRINTS IN THE SNOW

Driven from their cozy homes
Out into the cold dark night
Many without shoes to wear
What a terrible sight
Across the frozen ground they walked
Where to go they did not know
They left behind all that they owned
And bloody footprints in the snow

Across the frozen Mississippi
They walked on through the night
Frozen cold and hungry
Their hearts were filled with fright
Had their God forsaken them
They surely wondered so
But pushing ever onward
Leaving bloody footprints in the snow

But God had provided them
A place of safety up ahead
Though this terrible freezing night
Might leave many dead
They pushed on through the deadly cold
Fighting a terrible foe
Leaving their cozy homes behind
And bloody footprints in the snow.

WE ARE THANKFUL FOR A PROPHET

We are so very thankful
To have a prophet here on earth
To teach us of Savior
And how we can show our worth

By studying our scriptures
Through our humble prayer
Our prophet bares his testimony
That our Heavenly Father's there

He teaches us to live by faith
In our Father up above
He shows how we can know
Of His unconditional love

So we thank thee Father
For a prophet to lead the way
To teach of our Saviors love
Each and every day.

I guess you can tell that my thoughts have been much on the temple lately. It seems that you never know how much you miss something until it's really gone. Then you get a glimpse of that which was lost and suddenly you long for that one thing more than you ever did before. You suddenly realize how important that one thing was in your life and how you took it for granted when it was yours. This is how I felt after going to the temple for my son's wedding. The spirit I felt within those walls was like a long lost friend who I met after many years of separation. May we all pray that our temples will be open once again soon.

TALL WHITE SPIRE

When we see that tall white spire
With its angel shining bright
Our eyes are drawn to heaven
We think what a lovely sight
But do our thoughts turn to the truth
That lies within those walls
For the doorway to heaven
Is found in those sacred halls
For within the holy temple
We find the way back home
To be together with all of those
Who on earth no more do roam
We are joined together
In an unending chain of love
Back to our Heavenly Father
In His royal courts above.

UNENDING CHAIN OF LOVE

Imagine an ending chain
Stretching to eternity
Going back into the past
Farther than the eye can see
A never ending chain of ancestors
Who need our help today
To see that their work is done
So that they can find their way
Then looking forward to infinity
This great unbroken chain
Will forever show the love
That in our heart remains
Within the holy temple
Inside those sacred walls
This unending chain is linked
That not one soul shall fall

I HAVE MISSED THE TEMPLE

I have missed going to the temple
Feeling the spirit inside those walls
Seeing everyone dressed in white
As they walk those hallowed halls
Learning of creation
And of our Father's plan
Brought into fruition
For the betterment of man
Seeing a glimpse of eternity
And the beauty found therein
Leading us to salvation
That the battle we might win
But I know it will be a while
Then the House of the Lord
Will again be open
According to our Prophets word
Then once again we'll feel there
That spirit oh so sweet
When within those sacred walls
Once again we'll meet

WHEN TWO HEARTS ARE JOINED AS ONE

When two hearts are joined as one
In the temple of the Lord
They are sealed for all eternity
According to His word
Their love can grow by leaps and bounds
As they grow closer day by day
As they learn to live and love
Help each other along the way
With our Savior by their side
Through every trial they must face
Making home a heaven on earth
A bright and peaceful place
Working together to make it through
Walking always side by side
Hand in hand they'll go through life
And sweet will be the ride.

SONS OF MOSIAH

The sons of Mosiah
All good men and true
Refused to take the kingdom
For they knew what they should do
Go unto the Lamanites
To preach the gospel far and wide
That they might persuade them
That their words might turn the tide
Many were converted
By these brothers tall and strong
They became a faithful people
Who vowed to do no wrong
They buried up their weapons
Deep beneath the earth
Vowed never to take another's life
For all God's children have great worth
They became a righteous people
Filled with happiness and love
Blessed by our Heavenly Father
From His royal courts above